philosophy
works

philosophy
works

new light on life

PHILOSOPHY WORKS

Published by Arcturus Publishing Limited
26/27 Bickels Yard
151–153 Bermondsey Street
London SE1 3HA

First published 2006

ISBN-13: 978-1-84193-524-9
ISBN-10: 1-84193-524-7

Text © The School of Economic Science
Design Maki Ryan
Cover Design Peter Ridley

Printed in China

CONTENTS

FIRST THOUGHT

The purpose of *Philosophy Works* is to provide you with tools to allow you to begin the process of self-discovery. It will assist you in a reappraisal of the purpose and direction of your life. It will help you to meet life afresh.

Divided into ten steps, with seven reflections for each step, *Philosophy Works* provides a day-by-day process of transformation. The thoughts to be found in this book not only support the course from which they sprang, they also provide their own source of continuing inspiration for you to refer to over and over again.

Wisdom arises from experience rather than information. Use *Philosophy Works* in a practical way. Carry it with you. Refer to it. Apply what you read in all situations. Use it experimentally. Where there are directions see where they lead. Where there are questions consider the answers that arise.

Followed carefully, these ten steps will lead you to a deeper understanding of yourself and a re-inspired appreciation of life.

THE EXERCISE

At the heart of these ten steps in the development of a reflective attitude to life are two simple and yet powerful practices in awareness. The first one is called *The Exercise* and is more formal in nature. It needs to have time especially devoted to it twice a day. The Exercise is both ancient and entirely modern. It is both time honoured and of the moment. It is very simple and requires no special training.

Find a comfortable chair.

First let the mind be free of any concern or preoccupation.

Allow the body to be upright yet relaxed.

Let go of tension.
Be aware of where you are now...
Feel the body....
Feel the weight of the body on the
    chair....
Feel the gentle pressure of the
    clothes on the skin...
And the play of air on the face and
    hands...
See colour and form...
Be fully here...
And let listening be wide. Accept all
sounds.... those close at hand.... and
then those further and further away.....
Let all the sounds be held in the silent
listening, and rest in that awareness
for a minute or two.

THE PAUSE

The second reflective practice is far less formal and is called *The Pause*. It is to be practised in the midst of action, wherever you are regardless of your circumstances.

Come into the present by falling still and connecting mind with the senses. Be aware of colour, form, touch, taste, sound. Become aware of the underlying stillness and silence that lies beneath the surface of sensory perception. Rest there for a few moments before moving on to the next activity.

STEP ONE

WHY BE
WISE?

Socrates says an unexamined life is not worth living.

Philosophy asks you to consider the direction and meaning of your own life.

Start to ask yourself the important things like: 'Where does my life tend and to what end?'

Philosophy means the love of wisdom.

What does it mean to love wisdom, to feel passionate about truth and beauty?

Has life significance without these ideals?

Begin your search for the signs of wisdom however they might show themselves.

Begin to notice how your life is shaped
by the ideas that you hold.

Ask yourself: do these ideas tend
towards happiness, or do I entertain
destructive thoughts?

If so, how might they be dissolved?

Do you know anyone that's wise?

Look out for wisdom however it arises.

Consider what would a wise man or woman do in the situation you face.

Ask yourself: What are the qualities that the wise possess?

How might I remember them more often and make them central to my own life?

'Why is life so complicated?'
   Seek the simple solution by meeting
the moment fully and simply.

Rather than skidding across the surface of life, why not seek a more profound experience?

Bring into your life rest and depth.

Take time out, now. Even just for a moment by coming back to still moments.

Happy is the man that findeth wisdom, and the man that getteth understanding. For the merchandise of it is better than the merchandise of silver, and the gain thereof than fine gold. She is more precious than rubies: and all the things thou canst desire are not to be compared unto her.

Proverbs 3: 13-15

STEP TWO

REMAINING
TRUE TO
YOURSELF

What does it mean to remain true to yourself?

Take a note on one particular day of the mental and emotional changes that take place.

Constantly return to that which remains constant, and from a state of stillness observe all the changes in heart and mind.

Is it possible to fill an already full cup?
Remain open to new possibility.
Come into the present and be open
to what's on offer.

Consider the parts you play, and then rather than exhausting yourself by trying to seek an identity in those roles, stand back and enjoy the play.

Look, simply look; listen, simply listen.

Practise being in touch with what's before you.

Listen to what people have to say.

Be in touch with what the moment is asking.

Pursue an open door policy.
  Open eyes and ears.
  Open heart and mind.
  Rather than listening to
preconception, be open instead to what
the Now needs.

Work on self-knowledge is work on being.

Give yourself time to simply be rather than desperately trying to become something else.

*How can a soul which misunderstands
itself have a sure idea of other
creatures?*
Seneca

*Whoever knows essentially his own
nature, can know also that of another
man and can penetrate into the nature
of things. He can collaborate in
transformation.*
Confucius

This above all: to thine own self be true.
And it must follow, as the night the day.
Thou canst not then be false to any man.

Shakespeare

STEP THREE

LEVELS OF
AWARENESS

When you feel yourself transferred in
your imagination to another place or time
return to the here and now without delay.

Be conscious of your changing states of awareness.

Don't be identified with any of them.

Be conscious instead of what is it within you that remains unaffected.

By simple observation become more aware.

Nobody ever dreamed themselves into
a state of higher awareness.
  Steps towards greater
consciousness begin with an
appreciation of where you are now.
  Rest in self-awareness.
  Rest in the here-and-now.

From stillness open your mind to the great ideals.

Open your mind to beauty in particular.

You will not have to look far.

Nature is by nature never short of beauty.

Simply look.

Find beauty by looking.
Find beauty by listening.
Be in touch with beauty.
Taste it.
Be aware.

Notice that by being aware of beauty you become more still.

Notice that by becoming more still things begin to harmonize.

Notice that harmony is an expression of the unity that links us all.

Love is another great universal power.

Beauty, love, harmony, is there any difference in any of these?

Look for yourself.

Make up your own mind.

If you find a limit to your appreciation look again.

Love knows no measure, but is fervent above measure.

Love feels no burden, disdains no labours, would willingly do more than it can; complains not of impossibility because it conceives that it may and can do all things, where he that loveth not faints and lies down.

Love watches, and sleeping slumbers not; when weary is not tired, when straightened is not constrained; when frightened is not disturbed; but like a lovely flame and a torch all on fire, it moves upwards and securely passes through all opposition.

Whosoever loveth knoweth the sound of this voice.

Thomas à Kempis

STEP FOUR

TAPPING YOUR RESOURCES

When you show initiative, are good at problem solving and are quick witted in a tight situation, then you are said to be resourceful.

There is a knowledge that arises to meet the moment, but only when you're in the moment.

Access your resources by keep coming back.

Fear saps energy. It denudes you of vitality.

To live life to the full you have to be courageous.

Courage is said to be the first requirement of a philosopher.

Have the courage to keep laying aside your fears.

Gain strength by making connection.
    Outer connection comes by keen
attention.
    Inner arises from stillness.

We have the potential to meet the need.
Human intelligence allows us to do
that most creatively.
So be creative.
Meet the need by letting the universal
powers come to your aid.

Courage to begin with, willingness to seize the moment, generosity of spirit – which is love by another name – these are the universal powers.

Be a vehicle for their expression.

But fear, doubt, agitation are obstacles
to empowerment.

Be conscious of them creeping in
unnoticed.

Allow them to dissolve away by
serving wholeheartedly the situations
you meet.

Don't be tyrannised by negative emotion.

Turn and confront your fears.

However they might dress themselves up, they have nothing to do with what creation is asking.

When anger and fear, and pleasure and pain and jealousies and desires tyrannise over the soul – I call all this injustice.

Plato, Laws

There is no fear in love; but perfect love casteth out fear.

Jesus, St John 4:18

STEP FIVE

THE LIGHT
OF REASON

The wise are reasonable.
    In all the things you meet,
there is always a choice.
    Allow agitation to subside; fall still;
become calm; appeal to reason.

There is such a thing as the light of reason.

So rather than being caught up, step back into the cool, calm and dispassionate light of reason.

There is a difference between reason
and justification.
    Don't try to use reason to justify the
unreasonable.

Conscience and consciousness are closely related.

Find their relationship by allowing the conscious light of reason to indicate what is true and right.

When division and conflict arise look to resolve them by referring to the next wider unity: family, community, nation, humanity.

Be an agent of Reason whatever your sphere of influence.

Not true and right for me alone.

Reason suggests that the individual should care for the family, the family should care for the community, the community should care for the nation and the nation should care for humanity.

When you truly act reasonably you also love.

Both love and reason dissolve the divides and unify.

*If we have failed to understand,
it is that we have thought of knowledge
as a mass of theorems and an
accumulation of propositions.*

*But this is not wisdom built up of
theorems but one totality, not manifold
detail reduced to a unity, but rather a
unity working out into detail.*

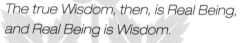

The true Wisdom, then, is Real Being,
and Real Being is Wisdom.

Plotinus, The Enneads V, viii, 4,5

STEP SIX

THE POWER
OF BEAUTY

Beauty has the power to transform your impression of life, but it will not impress itself upon you until you become aware of it.

Deliberately turn out and become conscious of beauty.

Be aware of the signs of it everywhere.

Find time to connect mind with the senses.

Without trying to cling onto anything, take pleasure in the world around you in all its variety.

See beauty in the unexpected.

Inspiration has its own beauty.

The words of the wise can be most inspiring.

Take one of the texts to be found in this book and deliberately appreciate its beauty.

Things done for the benefit of others
have beauty.
    Be conscious of them taking place.
    Perform them yourself.

In all this great variety of beautiful things, become conscious of what they hold in common.

Does beauty stand by itself, out there in the world, or does beauty within rise to meet outer beauty?

If inner beauty rises where does it come from, and how can it be encouraged to rise more often?

When we experience beauty are we made more separate, or does our heart go out?

Can beauty be discovered without love in some sense being there also?

Do we feel more at one with things when we both love and experience beauty?

One of the functions of art is undoubtedly to allow to us escape from the narrowness of our own vision and discover something of the breadth and depth, beauty and wholeness of life

Leonardo da Vinci - Notebooks

He who has been instructed thus far in the things of love, and who has learned to see the beautiful in due order and succession, when he comes towards the end will suddenly perceive a nature of wondrous beauty – a nature which in the first place is everlasting, knowing not birth or death, growth or decay:

secondly not fair in one point of view and foul in another…but beauty absolute, existing with itself, simple and everlasting, which is imparted to the ever growing and perishing beauties of all beautiful things, without itself suffering diminution, or increase, or any change.

Plato – Symposium

STEP SEVEN

'KNOW
THYSELF'

Be aware of the relationship between your thoughts and emotions and your physical state.

Be conscious of the impact heart and mind have on well-being.

Do your thoughts and emotions remain the same or are they constantly undergoing change?

Have you ever wondered who you really are?

Is the constantly changing the constant thing, or is there something observing all these changes?

What is it about yourself that has always been the same, from your earliest memories, despite all the things that have taken place over the years?

Are you more likely to find yourself
whilst caught up in all the usual
involvements, or will you discover more
in a stiller more composed state of mind?
Try them both and see for yourself.

What happens when you give your attention?

Open your mind to all that's around you.

And give your attention fully, without involvement, to the immediate task in hand.

Find strength in composure, energy in uninvolved attention, and in both find an indication of the most powerful qualities that you possess.

The ocean has both an agitated surface and still depths.

So does the mind.

Where are you more likely to discover both wisdom and self-awareness, on the agitated surface or in the still depths?

To me the very essence of education is the concentration of mind, not collection of facts. If I had to do my education again, I would not study facts at all. I would develop the power of concentration and detachment, and then, with a perfect instrument, collect facts at will.

Vivekananda – Education

STEP EIGHT

WATCHING THE POWERS AT WORK

We can be active and creative, steadfast and reliable, and there is that in us which remains still and peaceful.

It is the role of practical philosophy to enable us to access these powers and use them appropriately.

Movement and rest are seen in everything.

The cycle of action and inaction is familiar to us all.

Purposeful and effective action is dependent on knowing when to act.

Knowing when to act is dependent on inner stillness.

What are the states that rule heart and mind?

Are there times when you can't seem to get rid of mental agitation?

Are you sometimes overcome by lethargy?

What is available when your mind is clear?

Are you agitated or lethargic then, or is there a calm resource that allows you to be quietly effective?

Action has its place and so does rest, but what makes the difference in your ability to measure out exactly what's needed is connection with your own bright light of consciousness.

Use the Exercise to encourage a clear mind and an open heart.

What is it about you that stands back
and looks on?
   Rather than being possessed by your
involvements, return to conscious
awareness.
   Then look out of your own eyes.
   Listen through your own ears.
   To be truly in touch, step back.
   Try it and see.

At the moment you are about to be
sucked into the situations you face,
widen your view, embrace the whole,
respond, don't react.

Pleasure and pain are often associated with the body.

Our thinking is often ruled by the pursuit of one and the avoidance of the other.

The great teachers encourage us to rise above this duality, and rest instead in quiet observation.

'The wise man watches the movements of his mind.' Watch the movements of your own mind.

Observe where your thinking tends.

Our life is shaped by our minds; we become what we think.

Joy follows a pure thought like a shadow that never leaves.

Buddha – Dhamapada

STEP NINE

RENEWAL
THROUGH
REFLECTION

Work for stillness and lightness of being.

Adopt a more reflective approach to life.

Even in the midst of activity take time to stop and return to rest.

This is the way to find the right measure.

Rise refreshed from sleep.
　Then remain conscious of life by
avoiding slipping back into daydreams.

Observe the balance of the energies and when necessary take conscious steps to change the balance.

When it's time to rest, rest, but when it's time for action make it decisive and clear, not diffident and unfocussed.

In any situation what is more effective, stress-laden reaction or clear response?

Even when overwhelmed by events you may always detach yourself from your desperate involvements in order to return to the calm light of observation.

When agitation rules, is it easy to give
your attention?

When you are sluggish and dull, what
happens then?

Rather than either of these would it
not be better to simply rest attention
cleanly on the task in hand?

Better than desperately exhausting yourself, learn how a still and measured response to events offers its own energy.

Lightness of being, deftness of touch, clarity of thought, generosity of spirit – to be more conscious in your approach, constantly return to the Exercise.

Men seek seclusion in the wilderness, by the seashore, or in the mountains – a dream you have cherished only too fondly yourself.

But such fancies are wholly unworthy of a philosopher, since at any moment you choose whether you can retire within yourself.

Nowhere can a man find a quieter or more untroubled retreat than in his own soul....

Avail yourself often then, of this retirement, and so continually renew yourself.

Marcus Aurelius

Rather than desperately trying to become something else, would it not be better to work on being and discover in the process who you really are?

Between actions constantly come back to rest.

STEP TEN

INNER
REALITY